*Costumes of the
Nineteenth Century*

The YOUR BOOK Series

Acting	Fishes	Recorder
Aeromodelling	Flower Arranging	Rugger
Animal Drawing	Flower Making	The Seashore
Aquaria	Flying	Self-Defence
Astronomy	Freshwater Life	Sewing
Badminton	Furniture	Shell Collecting
Basketball	Golf	Skating
Bridges	Gymnastics	Soccer
Butterflies and Moths	Heraldry	Sound
Camping	Hockey	Space Travel
The Way a Car Works	Hovercraft	Squash
Card Games	The Human Body	Stamps
Card Tricks	Judo	Surnames
Chemistry	Kites	Survival Swimming
Chess	Knitting and Crochet	and Life Saving
Coin Collecting	Knots	Swimming
Computers	Landscape Drawing	Swimming Games and
Confirmation	Light	Activities
Contract Bridge	Lino-cutting	Table Tennis
Medieval and Tudor	Magic	Tape Recording
Costume	Maps and Map-	Television
17th & 18th Century	Reading	Tennis
Costume	Model Car Racing	Trampolining
19th Century Costume	Modelling	Trees
Dinghy Sailing	Money	Underwater Swimming
Diving	Music	Veteran and
The Earth	Paper Folding	Edwardian Cars
Electronics	Parliament	Vintage Cars
Embroidery	Party Games	Watching Wildlife
Engines and Turbines	Patience	Waterways
The English Bible	Pet Keeping	Weather
The English Church	Photography	Weaving
Fencing	Photographing Wildlife	Woodwork
Figure Drawing	Puppetry	The Year

People in Richmond Park. One lady wears a hat tied under the chin, the next has a spencer and the seated lady a poke bonnet. All have small neck ruffs. The gentleman has a frock coat and strapped trousers. *c.* 1822.

Costumes of the Nineteenth Century

PHILLIS CUNNINGTON

Publishers
PLAYS, INC.
Boston

ST. PHILIPS COLLEGE LIBRARY

*First published in 1970
by Faber and Faber Limited
3 Queen Square London WC1*

© *Phillis Cunnington 1970
Published in Great Britain under the title*
Your Book of Nineteenth Century Costume
*First American edition published by
Plays, Inc. 1970
Reprinted 1972*

Library of Congress Catalog Card Number
79-125605

International Standard Book Number
0-8238-0093-8

Printed in Great Britain

CONTENTS

MEN'S CLOTHES	*page* 7
WOMEN'S CLOTHES	25
The Classical Period	25
The Romantic Period	32
The Demure Period	41
The Extravagant Period	47
The Bustle Period	56
The Practical Period	67
CHILDREN'S CLOTHES	74
INDEX	78

MEN'S CLOTHES

All through the 19th century a man's suit consisted of a coat, waistcoat and trousers or sometimes breeches or knickerbockers. His wardrobe comprised a day suit, a dress suit and a sports suit.

During the first half of the century the coat, waistcoat and leg wear were often of different colours and different materials. A suit of the same colour and material was called 'a suit of dittos'. The two garments most typical of this century were the frock coat and the top hat (Fig. 1).

The collarless coat of the 18th century never returned to fashion.

The Coat

For the coat worn with the suit there were five main styles.
(1) *The Tail Coat* (Fig. 2), cut back in front at waist level to fall in two tails behind, was worn during the day till the 1830's, and continued for evening dress to the end of the century (Fig. 3).
(2) *The Morning Coat* had the front edges of the coat made to slope back from waist level to shorter tails behind (Fig. 4).
(3) *The Frock Coat* came into fashion in 1816 and lasted to the end of the 19th century. It was derived, soon after Waterloo, from a military coat. It was something like a well-fitting overcoat generally ending above the knee (see Fig. 1).
(4) *The Jacket* was worn by gentlemen from the 1840's,

Men's Clothes

1. Frock coats as worn indoors and outdoors: (a) with strapped pantaloons, 1830, (b) holding top hat, 1830's.

though earlier by workmen. At first it was slightly waisted but from the 1850's it usually hung straight down like a blazer and, being loose and comfortable, was often called a *lounging jacket* or a *lounge* (Fig. 5).

(5) *The Norfolk Jacket*, a new kind of lounge, started in the 1860's. It had box pleats back and front and a belt of the same material. It was worn with knickerbockers for sport and in the country (Fig. 6).

Men's Clothes

2. Men wearing strapped trousers: (a) in tail coat, (b) in frock coat. Lady in poke bonnet and shawl, 1838.

The Waistcoat or 'Vest'

This was now sleeveless, except for the type worn by some workers and later railway porters. At first, it had collar and lapels, but these were largely discarded in the 1870's and it was then known as a 'straight' waistcoat. Like the coats it could be single-breasted or double-breasted; but until the

Men's Clothes

3. Evening-dress suit, 1865.

4. Morning coat, 1894.

1890's evening-dress waistcoats were single-breasted; then the double-breasted form became correct.

In the 1890's, especially for evening dress, waistcoats were being replaced by the *Cummerbund*. This was a wide sash of black or coloured silk which was wound round the waist and fastened on one side. It was reported in August 1893 that Mr. Austen Chamberlain was seen in the House of Commons wearing: 'a waistband of broad stripes of blazing yellow and red silk.'

Men's Clothes

5. (a) Lounge jacket in velveteen, 1867, (b) Gardener in jacket and breeches, 1807.

Leg Wear

(1) *Trousers* began to be fashionable in 1807. The front fastening, at first, was made by a turn-down flap called a *fall*. The fly front (buttons concealed under a fold) started in 1823 and was usual from then on.

Between 1820 and 1850 *strapped trousers*, that is trousers strapped under the shoe like gaiters, were fashionable (see Figs. 2a and 2b).

Men's Clothes

6. Norfolk jacket, 1891.   7. Waistcoat with watch pocket, strapped pantaloons, 1828.

(2) *Railroad Trousers* was the name given to trousers made of material with vertical stripes like railway lines.

(3) *Peg-Top Trousers* were wide above, sloping down to a close fit at the ankles (1857–65). Perhaps as a result of prudery, to talk of trousers was considered vulgar and some extra-

Men's Clothes

ordinary names were given to them, such as 'unmentionables', 'inexpressibles', 'unwhisperables', 'nether integuments' and others.

(4) *Pantaloons* were worn as a change from trousers all through the first half of this century. They were close-fitting and often called 'tights'. They were secured by straps under the foot like the strapped trousers (Fig. 7).

(5) *Breeches* (Fig. 8), also called 'small clothes', went out of fashion for day wear after about 1830, but continued to be worn for court or ceremonial dress and also for country walks and certain sports and by working men to the end of the century (Fig. 9).

Braces were worn with all leg wear, and had buttons for their attachment. They were often embroidered by ladies as presents for their men friends, as:

'A pair from Mary worked with an ecclesiastical pattern.' 1853.

Neck Wear

All through the first half of the century shirt collars were very high and neck ties or neck cloths, as they were called, were large and usually white. A lady in 1800 wrote:

'Pray is it the fashion for the shirt collar to stand as high as the corners of the eyes?'

There were two main types of neck ties:

(1) *The Stock.* This was a made-up stiffened neckband fastened behind. After 1830 it was mainly worn for sport.

(2) *The Cravat.* This was scarf-like and spread out over the shirt in front, where it might be fixed with a tie pin, or tied in a bow.

8. Country suit, 1899.

Men's Clothes

10. An Octagon Tie, 1890.

9. Letter collector before the days of pillar boxes. He wears a red coat with blue lapels and buff breeches, 1824.

As a protest against the discomfort of these scarves a few eccentrics began to wear 'a wisp of black silk round the neck' and in the 1840's these small cravats were called 'Byron ties' from the poet's liking for them.

By the 1860's shirt collars were lowered and either turn-down or stand-up, and neck ties were small and tied in a bow, and later a knot. Larger specimens were made up and fastened behind, spreading out in front, such as the *octagon tie* (Fig. 10). See the *Bab Ballads*, *c.* 1868:

Men's Clothes

With a hat all awry
And an octagon tie
And a miniature, miniature glass in his eye.

Outdoor Garments

The Great Coat was the most important. It varied in shape and length and was given many different names:

The *Surtout* and the *Paletot* were fairly short overcoats appearing *c.* 1820 and 1830.

The *Frock Great Coat* or *Top Frock,* as it came to be called, was like a long frock coat.

The *Box Coat* had one or more capes and was worn by coachmen and travellers on a coach.

The *Chesterfield* was very popular from the 1840's on. It had a velvet collar and plenty of pockets, including a small ticket pocket, added in 1859 (Fig. 11a).

The *Inverness* appeared too in 1859 and was very popular to the end of the century. It had a deep cape which, from the 1870's, was incomplete behind, being sewn to the side seams (Fig. 11b).

The *Mackintosh* arrived on the scenes in 1836. It was an overcoat made of Mackintosh's patent India rubber cloth. Unfortunately it had a nasty smell and complaints were made when men wore them on buses 'on account of the offensive stench which they emit'.

The *Ulster*, which appeared in 1869, had a cape or a hood at first. In the 1870's a ticket pocket was put in the left sleeve.

Cloaks were also worn in the country or for walking, but were not town wear except for funerals (see Fig. 12).

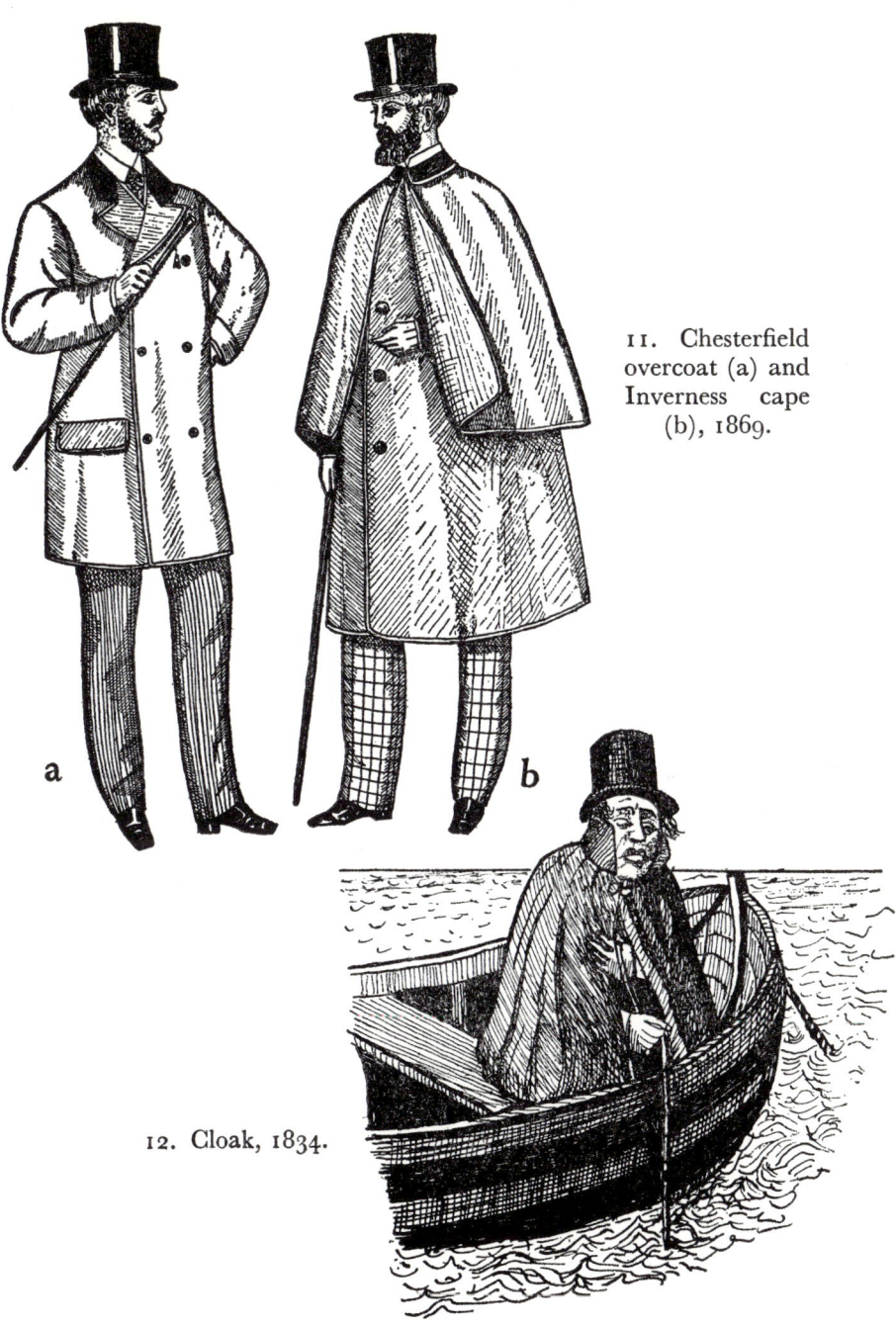

11. Chesterfield overcoat (a) and Inverness cape (b), 1869.

12. Cloak, 1834.

Men's Clothes

Evening-dress cloaks were always smart and made of rich materials.

Foot Wear

Boots were chiefly worn for riding and walking (Fig. 13).
Top boots ended just below the knees with a wide turn-down top of a lighter shade (Fig. 16).
Wellington boots, which appeared in 1819, were like top boots without the turn-over tops.
Hessians rose to a point just below the knee cap and were there decorated with a tassel. They were usually worn with pantaloons, but went out of fashion in the 1850's.
Highlows covered the ankles and were laced or fastened with a buckle and strap in front. They were popular with working men.

In the 1830's a number of short boots came into fashion. These were as follows:
Elastic-sided boots. These had gussets of India-rubberized material on each side. (Elastic had been patented in 1820.)
Button boots became correct town wear from 1837 and when made of patent leather were worn with evening dress from the 1870's. At this date highlows were a little more elegant, hence the quotation from *H.M.S. Pinafore*:

'Highlows pass as patent leathers.'

All through this century boots were correct for town wear and were always black.
Shoes were rarely worn out of doors. They were worn indoors as slippers and either laced up or tied over a central tongue. They, too, were always black until the 1890's when the *Tailor*

Men's Clothes

and Cutter announced that 'russet shoes are correct wear with sac and lounges', i.e. casual wear.

Overshoes in the form of rubber galoshes were introduced in 1842—the first waterproof foot wear.

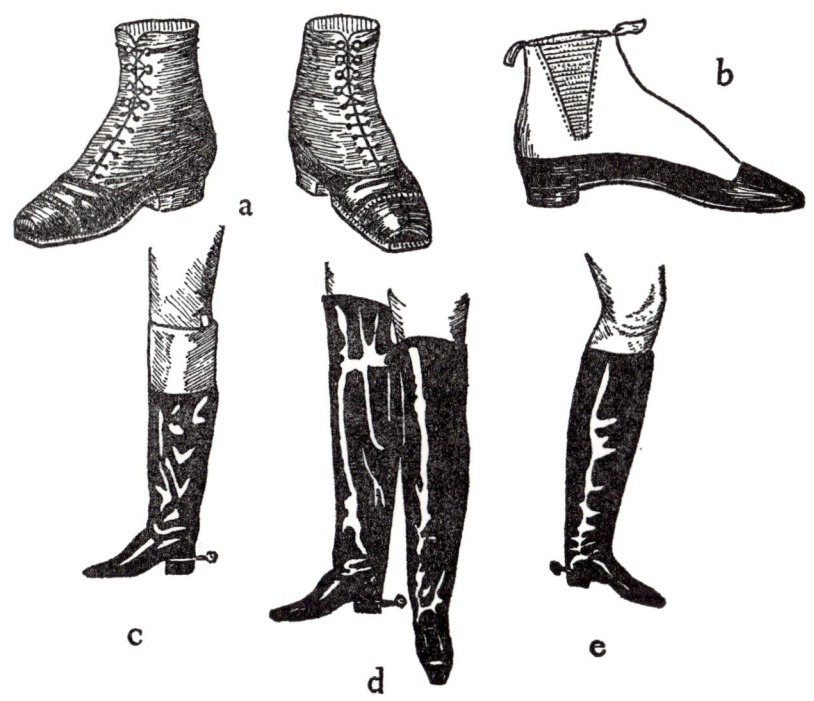

13. Boots: (a) laced up, (b) elastic side, the rest, various styles of top boots.

With evening dress *pumps* were worn. They were open over the instep, often just covering the toes, and there tied with a ribbon bow.

Gaiters

Long gaiters called 'spatterdashes', ending just below the knee,

Men's Clothes

were buttoned down the outside or centre and worn with breeches for country wear and hunting.

Half gaiters, called 'spats', were ankle length and went with pantaloons and trousers. White or fawn spats were town wear and correct with frock coats from 1893. Brown ones were favoured by dustmen and many artisans.

Head Wear

During this century gentlemen never went bare-headed out of doors.

The *Top Hat* was the most important for town wear. Because of its tall crown it was sometimes called a 'chimney-pot hat'. The brim was narrow. From *c*. 1830 it became a 'silk hat' and was black and shiny, but grey and brown were sporting varieties, and white was fashionable in the 1830's and 1840's. The *Bowler Hat* appeared in the 1860's. It was a hard felt with a dome-shaped crown and narrow brim (Fig. 14). It was usually black, but brown and fawn were worn with Norfolk jackets.

The less formal hats:

The *Wide-awake* of straw or felt, with a low crown and wide brim, was popular.

The *Bollinger* was a hard felt with a bowl-shaped crown with a knob on the top and a circular brim. It was first worn by cab drivers, but adopted by gentlemen through the 1850's and 1860's (Fig. 15).

The *Muffin Hat* was a soft cloth hat with a flat crown and narrow upturned brim. It was very popular for windy days.

The *Homburg* was a stiff felt with a dent along the crown from front to back. It was patronized by the Prince of Wales.

The *Trilby* was similar but of soft felt.

Men's Clothes

The *Straw Hat* or *Boater* (see Fig. 5a) was extremely popular and even worn in town in the 1890's, during the summer. A paper wrote in 1894:

'It was only last summer that Londoners began to wear straw hats with any freedom . . . it is straw-hattier than ever.'

14. Man in lounge suit and bowler hat. Woman in jacket bodice and apron-fronted overskirt. Hair flowing loose, an American fashion, 1873.

Men's Clothes

15. Seaside costumes. One man wears a bollinger and waisted jacket, the other a top hat and loose jacket, 1864.

Men's Clothes

Evening-dress Hats

The *Opera Hat* was crescent-shaped, and generally flattened from side to side so as to be carried under the arm. It was known as the 'Chapeau bras'.

The *Circumfolding Hat*, used after 1830, was a soft round hat which could also be squashed flat and put under the arm.

The *Gibus*, from the 1840's, was a top hat which could be treated in the same way, having springs in the lining of the crown.

Caps were only worn for sport or in the country. (See Fig. 8.) A fashion article in 1830 wrote of caps:

> 'These seem of late to have fallen entirely into disuse except for boys, the lower orders and the Services.'

The *Deer Stalker*, now associated with Sherlock Holmes, had peaks fore and aft and ear flaps tied together over the crown when not in use.

Hair

Wigs were worn by the elderly for a few years and by the legal profession throughout the century, but the general wearing of wigs ended with the 18th century.

At first, close curls, with a side or centre parting and a clean-shaven face, were the fashion. Whiskers were the mode from the 1820's on, sometimes with short beards.

In the 1890's a short cut was correct, and anyone whose hair was a trifle long was called a poet or a musician trying to imitate Tennyson or Paderewski.

Moustaches were often worn after the Crimean War, appearing about 1857, and beards were common from the 1870's, but with older men only.

Men's Clothes

Long hair was never fashionable with the 'top people', but Dickens, in the *Pickwick Papers*, describes a solicitor's clerk in 1837 as 'winding his hair round the brim of his hat as he came along'.

Accessories

Gloves were essential in town. They were usually of brown doeskin or kid. Coloured gloves were sometimes worn and in 1859 city clerks were described as 'dashing young parties who purchase pea-green, orange and rose-pink gloves'.

Evening gloves were white kid.

Sticks or *Canes* were usually carried by gentlemen, probably symbolizing the 18th-century sword.

Umbrellas gradually became more fashionable than canes. Beau Brummell's umbrella in 1832 was 'of brown silk, always protected by a silk case; the handle surmounted by the head of Geo. IV carved in ivory'.

In the 1880's the umbrella had to be rolled up as tightly as possible; this was correct and woe to the gentleman if he had to disturb it.

WOMEN'S CLOTHES
The Classical Period (1800—1820)

Dresses

Dresses during this period were supposed to imitate Greek statuary and the silhouette was like a pillar. Accordingly the dress had a high waist-line and full-length straight-hanging skirt with or without a train (Fig. 16).

Flimsy materials were often used in order to show off the shape of the body. A journal in 1800 wrote:

'Females are almost as naked as Mother Eve before the fall.'

The *Frock* for day or evening was buttoned behind and the *Chemise Robe* was buttoned in front from neck to hem. The *Tunic Dress* was evening wear. It had a tunic worn over a frock, round or trained, but the tunic was shorter than the frock (Fig. 17).

For Court wear the huge hooped skirt of the eighteenth century survived, but was discontinued after 1820 as George IV didn't like it.

A curious freak fashion lasting from 1815 to 1819 was the 'Grecian Bend' when a forward stoop was considered fashionable. To increase this effect a small bustle was worn under the skirt, high up. This posture was repeated in 1868.

Women's Clothes

16. Lady in high-waisted dress and mob cap. Man in tail coat and top boots with tabs for pulling on, 1815.

17. Evening dress with draped tunic, 1811.

Neck Wear

By day half-handkerchiefs could be worn, loosely tied round the neck. Small ruffs were fashionable until the 1830's and revived in the 1870's. A 'tucker' was a strip of lace worn to fill in the front of a very low-cut bodice.

The Classical Period

18. Pelisse, winter walking costume, 1807.

19. White muslin pelisse and dress. Summer walking costume, 1819.

Outdoor Garments

The *Pelisse* was a long, short-waisted overcoat (Figs. 18 and 19).

The *Spencer* was a short jacket, pulled in to fit round the short waist (Fig. 20 and frontispiece).

The *Cloak* or *Mantle* (Fig. 21) was either an ordinary cloak

Women's Clothes

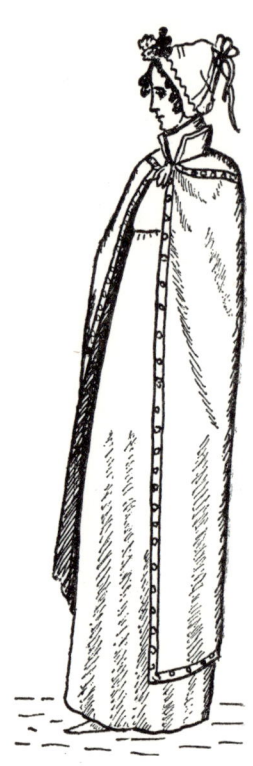

20. Spencer, 1820.   21. Cloak, 1807.

with or without an attached hood, or it was a cape with long ends hanging down in front on either side.

The *Shawl* was large or small but in this period not too popular. A fashion writer in 1806 said of the shawl:

'It is wonderful that the shawl should ever have found its path to fashionable adoption. . . . It is the very contrast to the flowing elegance of Grecian costume.'

The Classical Period

Large *Muffs* of fur, feathers or satin trimmed with swansdown were very popular.

Foot Wear

Indoors

Shoes or slippers with short uppers and flat heels could be of leather or silk or velvet matching the dress.
Sandals were tied over the instep or had criss-cross lacing up the front and were then generally called Roman sandals.

Outdoors

Half Boots reaching to the calf were laced in front or sometimes behind or at the side or buttoned. For 'carriage exercise' they might be made of silk, satin or velvet.
Highlows like those worn by men were worn by girls in the country.
Pattens used with other foot gear were wooden soles raised on iron rings as a protection from muddy roads.
Gaiters were sometimes worn.
Stockings, black, white or coloured, were held up by garters made of narrow strips of knitted wool tied above or below the knee.

Head Wear

Indoors

Day. The *Mob Cap* was usual, made of cambric, puffed out and gathered into a band, edged with a frill (see Fig. 16).
Evening. Lace caps, bonnets, small hats trimmed with feathers and all sorts of ornaments were fashionable.

Outdoors

Hats had low crowns and wide brims until *c.* 1814 when crowns shot up high and brims were narrowed.

Women's Clothes

The popular *Gipsy Hat* was tied under the chin by ribbon passing over the crown.

Bonnets resembled the hats but had no brim at the back and were always tied under the chin. The poke bonnet had a brim poking forward (see frontispiece) and was worn beyond this period. It was not liked by a gentleman who wrote in 1822:

'Another street nuisance is your poke bonnet—ladies who sometimes put out your eyes with these pent-house projections.'

One curious rule dictated by fashion all through the 19th century was that some kind of head gear must always be worn out of doors, both by men and women, especially by women. Here is an interesting quotation from a novel by Disraeli in 1837:

' "But you must get a bonnet, Henrietta; I must forbid your going out uncovered."

' "No, papa, this will do," said Miss Temple, taking a handkerchief, twisting it round her head and tying it under her chin.

' "You look like an old woman, Henrietta," said her father smiling.'

What would he have thought of us today?

Hair

Hair was arranged with a mass of curls on top with ringlets falling at the back, or with short curls all over. Wigs worn over a short crop were common during the first ten years of this century.

The Classical Period

Make-up

Rouge was 'all the rage and without your cheeks were the colour of a peony you were not à la mode'.

Referring to an elderly lady, Sir Walter Elliot, in Jane Austen's *Persuasion*, says:

'Morning visits are never fair by women at her time of life who make themselves up so little. If she would only wear rouge she would not be afraid of being seen.' 1818.

WOMEN'S CLOTHES
The Romantic Period (1820's and '30's)

This was a gay period. In contrast to the earlier styles it was picturesque rather than statuesque and the outline no longer vertical, but wide above and below.

Dresses

By day, gowns without trains were usual, with long or ankle-length skirts. The waist came down to its normal level by 1824 and a buckled belt or sash was usual.

Sleeves were puffed out, the largest being the 'leg of mutton' or 'gigot' sleeve (Fig. 22). It was very distended in 1830 but collapsed after 1836.

Although this sleeve was the height of fashion, a lady in 1825 wrote:

'Don't let Caroline adopt the sleeve à gigot. It is frightful for a thin arm and absurd for a fat one.'

Evening Dresses

These were similar to the day styles but more heavily trimmed and generally

22. White morning dress with 'leg of mutton' sleeves, buckled sash and black satin shoes. Indoor cap, trimmed with lace and ribbon, 1824.

The Romantic Period

23. Court or evening dress with beret sleeves, large turban head dress, 1830.

Women's Clothes

very décolleté. This amusing rhyme was written in 1825:

> *When dress'd for the evening the girls nowadays*
> *Scarce an atom of dress on them leave*
> *Nor blame them—for what is an evening dress*
> *But a dress that is suited for Eve?*

Sleeves were short and in the 1830's they spread out on each side and were known as 'beret sleeves' (Fig. 23).

A bustle, consisting of a pad stuffed with wool, was sometimes worn behind. Perhaps this helped women to appear plump, which was fashionable at the time.

Outdoor Garments

The *Pelisse* was now a figure-fitting coat, sometimes having one or more capes. In summer it might be sleeveless because of the difficulty of wearing it over gigot sleeves.

The *Mantle* was a long cloak often having a deep cape (Fig. 24).

Shawls were still worn (Fig. 25).

Fur tippets (capes) and large muffs were winter wear.

Foot Wear

Indoors

Slippers with flat heels and ribbon sandals were worn for parties. Black satin slippers were correct for evening wear.

Outdoors

Boots with cloth or velvet uppers and leather for the shoe part were usual.

Gaiters were worn in cold weather.

24. Velvet mantle, trimmed and lined with swansdown, 1824.

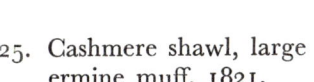

25. Cashmere shawl, large ermine muff, 1821.

Women's Clothes

Head Wear

Indoors
Day. Bonnet-shaped white caps with starched frills and ribbon ties, often left dangling, were gay and very fashionable.
Many caps were trimmed with artificial flowers.
The plain mob cap disappeared into the kitchen.
Evening. Fancy turbans and berets, variously trimmed with ribbons, flowers and feathers shooting upwards, were fashionable, but perhaps the most popular was the evening-dress hat wired up into fantastic shapes and loaded with trimming. A gentleman at dinner seated between two of them complained that he only 'caught an occasional glance of (his) plate' (see Fig 23).

Outdoors
Bonnets were gaining the day over hats. Crowns were tall and brims were large, curving high round the face. The 'bavolet' was a short curtain or frill at the back to shade the neck, added from 1830 on. Many had white frills sewn to the insertion of the bonnet strings which, when tied, formed a white frill round the chin. These were called 'chin-stays' or 'Mentonnières' (Fig. 26).
Hats were large and heavily trimmed (Fig. 27). They were made of silk or satin and many were of straw. The *Manchester Iris* in 1823 stated that:

'There were 136,045 leghorn straw hats imported into Great Britain' (see Fig. 28).

Large black veils were worn with bonnets and hats and often thrown back over the shoulders as a gay gesture.

The Romantic Period

26. Man in military frock coat. Woman with gigot sleeves and wearing a bonnet with mentonnières, 1827.

Women's Clothes

27. Fashionable dress and hat, 1828.

Hair

This usually had a centre parting with curls each side, and the back hair was twisted into a bun on top. For evening wear a few ringlets fell loose on the neck behind. A distinctive feature from 1824 to the 1830's was the *Apollo Knot*. It consisted of two or three loops of false hair wired up to stand erect on top of the head (Fig. 29). Since a cap could not be

The Romantic Period

28. Straw hat trimmed with feathers. Neck ruff, 1820.

29. Evening dress and Apollo knot hair style, 1828.

worn with this, flowers or lace decorations were always added.

Make-up

Rouge was not fashionable as pale faces were thought more romantic.

Women's Clothes

Accessories

Coloured gloves for day and white kid ones for evening were correct.

Handbags called reticules were small silk, satin or velvet bags closed by a draw-string. Since dresses had no pockets these were essential.

Parasols were very fashionable. A journal in 1823 wrote:

'It is the fashion now not to hold up the parasol for it only prevents the men getting a glimpse of us, but merely to carry it dangling in the hand to show you've got one.'

WOMEN'S CLOTHES
The Demure Period (1840's)

Dresses

Dresses now had pinched-in waists, drooping shoulders and long skirts (see Fig. 30).

Day dresses were made in one with a boned bodice hooked up behind, or else a *jacket bodice* was worn, soon after 1846. This was figure fitting and spread out over the hips, but was longer for riding costumes (Fig. 31). Sleeves were tight or slightly bell-shaped. The fullness of the dome-shaped skirt was produced by a bustle and a petticoat made of crinoline material, besides two flannel and two cotton petticoats. In 1848 someone wrote:

'No doubt our present long waists and immense wide skirts may appear very puzzling to a future generation.'

Evening dresses

A curious economy was practised in having the same skirt for a day or an evening bodice. These were always made to match. Round the low neck a deep falling border of lace frills and ribbon was a favourite addition. It was called a 'Bertha' (Fig. 32).

Short white gloves were correct after 1844.

Women's Clothes

30. Day dress, 1843.

31. Jacket bodice of riding costume, 1843.

Outdoor Garments

The main garments were:
The *Shawl*.
The *Pelerine* was only a long or short cape.
The *feather pelerine*, made by hand with farmyard feathers, was a novelty. A beautiful specimen can be seen at the Gallery of English Costume, Manchester.
The *Pardessus* (Fig. 33a) was a figure-fitting long jacket.

32. Evening dress, 1847.

33. (a) and (b) Carriage costumes: (a) wears a white silk 'pardessus'. Both have very demure bonnets, 1849.

Women's Clothes

Foot Wear

This continued as in the previous section.
India-rubber galoshes were introduced in 1842. In a letter to a lady in 1847 the Duke of Wellington wrote:

'The India-rubber galoshes will keep your feet dry.'

Evening boots, coloured or white, were fashionable from 1847.

Head Wear

Indoors
Day. Small white caps, not tied under the chin.
Evening. White caps richly trimmed: some had lace lapels, i.e. pendants hanging down each side.
Hats were rare and young women preferred some sort of head decoration only.

Outdoors
Bonnets with a narrow brim curving round the face were the rule. Trimming was moderate, but was sometimes added all round the inside of the brim, framing the face.
An extra brim, called an *Ugly*, appeared in 1848. It was made of silk stretched over loops of cane and was tied on over the bonnet brim to shade the face from the sun. It could be folded flat when not in use.
  Hats were small and not often used, but they were worn for riding, and some women wore a top hat on horseback.

The Demure Period

Hair

Day and *Evening*

Hair styles were very demure (Fig. 34). From a centre parting the hair was combed smoothly down on each side and then plaited into a circle covering the ears or spread out over the ears and twisted back to join a bun behind. Long side ringlets were also worn, chiefly with evening dress. These curls were often bought ready-made and fixed to combs for easy adjustment (Fig. 35).

34. Hair style, *c.* 1840.

35. Hair style for evening dress, *c.* 1842.

Women's Clothes

Accessories

Make-up was out.
Reticules were less used, as skirts now had pockets.

Foot Wear

Fig. 36 shows foot wear from 1800 to the 1840's.

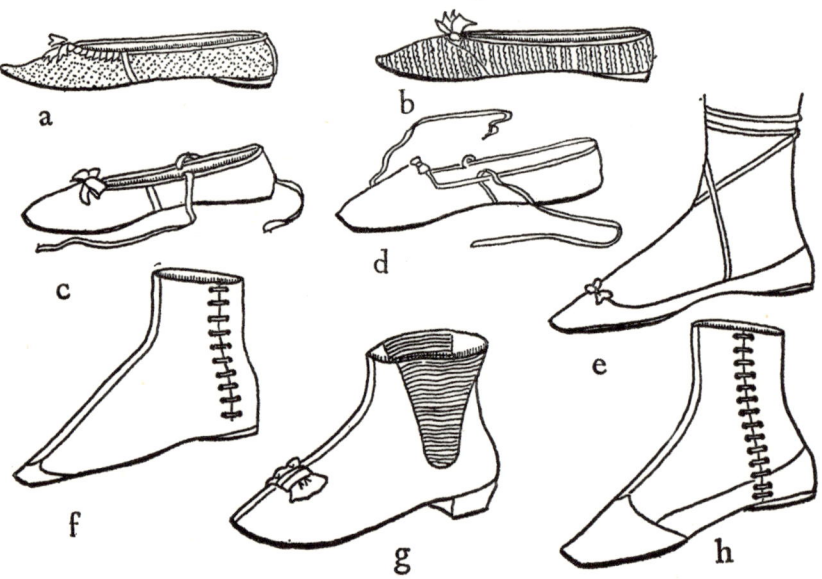

36. Boots and shoes worn from 1800 to 1840's.

WOMEN'S CLOTHES
The Extravagant Period (1850's and '60's)

England was now very prosperous, so Mrs. Fashion became extravagant and the amount of material used for each costume was enormous. Skirts in the middle 60's were the widest of all.

Dresses

Day

The bodice was separate from the skirt, generally ending with a round waist covered with a belt or a sash. Jacket bodices too were popular (see Fig. 37b), and a blouse and skirt costume was introduced for casual wear in the 1860's.

Sleeves were often bell-shaped, widening round the elbow and there filled in to the wrist by white detachable under-sleeves. Bishop sleeves were popular for blouses and the coat sleeve was common from 1863. Nearly all sleeves, especially in the 1860's, had epaulettes.

Skirts from 1856 were enormously distended over the *cage crinoline* (Fig. 38). This was a petticoat made of whalebone or watch-spring hoops. Crinolines took their name from the textile of horsehair and wool that was originally used to make them, but the name continued even afterwards. For walking, the skirt was often hitched up to show a scarlet under-petticoat shortened for exercise. But for country walks skirts of this period were not convenient. An inquirer in 1858 was told:

'not to attempt the climbing of stiles in a crinoline for the task is impossible; and if she suffers much from the comments of vulgar little boys, it would be better, in a high wind, to remain indoors'.

To avoid such difficulties an American lady, Mrs. Bloomer,

a   b

37. Skirts hitched up over crinolines: (a) shows a pork-pie hat, (b) a jacket bodice, 1863.

The Extravagant Period

38. Large crinoline, 1858.

tried, in 1851, to persuade English women to wear trousers. The kind she advocated were loose with a frill round the ankle, and were nicknamed bloomers (Fig. 39). Very few ladies, however, were daring enough to adopt them.

Evening dresses
These were like day wear, but always with short sleeves and very low-necked. In the 1860's the skirt was slightly trained and draped over-skirts were popular.

Women's Clothes

Outdoor Garments

Cloaks or *Mantles* and shawls were all worn, being convenient over the spreading skirts (Fig. 40a).

The *paletot* was a very full jacket shaped to spread over the crinoline skirt (Fig. 40b).

Loose jackets varying in length were worn by young women.

39. Lady in bloomers, 1853.

Foot Wear

Indoors

Shoes and slippers with low uppers and low heels continued. White satin or silk was usual for evening wear though in the 1860's they were often coloured to match the dress.

Outdoors

Boots were usual, either laced up on the inner side, buttoned on the outer, or else elastic sided.

Stockings with shoes were generally white; with boots they were coloured.

For riding, *Wellington boots* were correct.

Riding-habit skirts (no crinoline of course) were extremely

The Extravagant Period

long, as it was improper to show the legs (Fig. 41). A fashion article stated in 1867:

'In a fast gallop it is almost impossible to help showing the feet and when proper Wellington boots are not worn this is certainly not pretty.'

40. (a) Cloak, 1869, (b) Paletot, 1864.

Women's Clothes

41. Riding jacket and long habit skirt. Small hat, 1858.

Head Wear

Indoors

Day. White caps trimmed with ribbon streamers or small half handkerchiefs, often worn with the point forwards, were favourites with matrons, but fashion made a big concession in 1857 when it announced that:

'young married ladies need not wear caps until they acquire the endearing name of "Mother" '.

Young girls, however, were already replacing caps by ribbons

The Extravagant Period

and in the 1860's by the chignon. This was a mass of real or false hair often covered by a net and worn at the back of the head. The net was made of black silk or chenille, often decorated with beads.

Evening. Small richly trimmed caps, flowers, jewelled combs, diadems and velvet coronets were all the mode.

Outdoors

Bonnets in the 1850's were small and worn far back (Fig. 42a). From 1860-4 by far the most popular was the *Spoon bonnet* in

42. (a) Bonnet worn far back, 1853; (b) morning cap, 1856; (c) large straw hat, 1855; (d) small hat, 1866; (e) 'Ugly' worn over spoon bonnet, 1862; (f) spoon bonnet, 1864.

Women's Clothes

which the brim rose up above the forehead in a spoon-shaped curve; it gave no shade to the face, so the *ugly* was often added (Fig. 42e).

Hats. Wide straw hats were liked in the 1850's. The hats were smaller in the 1860's and the round *pork-pie* hat and the *Scotch Glengarry* were favourites. Trimming was moderate but ribbon streamers hanging down behind were conspicuous and popularly known as 'follow-me-lads'.

There was a curious convention about hats at this time; they were not to be worn on Sundays and never, no never, in church. Bonnets only were correct.

Veils continued.

Hair

Hair styles in the 1850's continued as in the 1840's. The chignon dominated the 1860's and the back hair gradually climbed up to the top of the head. Curls were often added for evening dress. *Punch* disliked the huge chignons and wrote in 1869:

'Modern chignons give a truly frightful shape to female heads.'

An American style occurring in the same year was to let the hair hang down loose over the shoulders.

Make-up

If used this must not be obvious; it was ungenteel. But young women did not always agree, as in 1868:

'At a recent public assembly every third woman seemed to

The Extravagant Period

be painted and eyebrows and eyelashes coloured, and false hair worn.'

Accessories

Curious earrings in the form of insects, fishes, ladders and even croquet mallets were worn. Croquet was now a very popular game for women.

Aprons were worn with home dresses. Some very small black silk aprons, sometimes embroidered, were called 'Fig leaves'.

WOMEN'S CLOTHES
The Bustle Period (1870's and '80's)

Extravagance continued and, owing to the help of the sewing-machine, dresses were more complicated than ever before. A fashion writer said:

'It is now quite impossible to describe dresses with exactitude ... the task of writing down how it is all made remains hopeless.'

The general outline was a tightly corseted bodice with a skirt flattened in front and puffed out behind. In the 1870's this was done by a crinolette, something like a small crinoline with hoops at the back only. From 1882 to 1889 the huge bustle was used instead. There were four years in between from *c.* 1878 to 1882 when dresses were tight all the way down, sheath-like and trained and having ties under the skirt to pull back and flatten the front. These dresses were known as 'tie-backs'. A gentleman wrote in 1878:

'It grates upon the common sense of every thinking man when he sees a fashionable lady waddling along, barely able to move her feet six inches at a time.'

All elegant dresses were heavily trimmed with ribbon, paste spangles, tinsel and sometimes, in the 1880's, with stranger forms of decoration such as artificial beetles, lizards, rats, mice, spiders, centipedes, etc. A magazine in 1884 asked

The Bustle Period

if cats, dogs and monkeys were suitable as dress trimmings and added:

'What shall we say of a dress trimmed with cat's heads, ditto her bonnet and muff?'

A mixture of colours too was very fashionable and *Punch* wrote in 1876:

43. (a) Dress with jacket bodice, 1870, (b) Norfolk jacket worn with tie-back trained skirt, 1878.

Women's Clothes

'Neither flowers nor rainbows can show such colours as are worn now by our fashionable girls.'

Dresses

Day

The *House dress*, however, was plain and consisted of a skirt and a matching blouse, jacket bodice or Norfolk jacket; the latter could even go with a trained skirt! (See Fig. 43.)

44. (a) Princess Polonaise dress, 1876, (b) 'Dolly Varden' costume, 1871.

The Bustle Period

The *Princess dress* had a fitting bodice which was continued down like a tunic, making an over-skirt.

The *Princess Polonaise*—very popular—was similar, having the over-skirt looped up on one side (Fig. 44a).

The 'Dolly Varden' dress (Fig. 44b) was a variation of this style, and was worn by all classes (see Dickens's *Barnaby Rudge*).

Sleeves generally were close-fitting to the wrist or just above. Epaulettes went out of fashion soon after 1870.

Skirts. All fashionable skirts were double or draped or trimmed to imitate an over-skirt. The apron-fronted style was very common (see Figs. 45 and 14). In the '70's women even played tennis in trains. Some skirts in the 1880's were designed for exercise and these were fully pleated behind and had no over-skirt but they still reached the feet.

There was one comfortable dress which was allowed indoors, the *Teagown*. It was something like a grand dressing-gown and was worn without corsets. Caps were imperative with this. But it was ruled that:

'young ladies are not expected to wear teagowns as this apparel is reserved for the married'.

Evening dresses

These were always very décolleté and trained (Fig. 46). They had short sleeves, puffed or plain, and trimming was very lavish (Fig. 47). A magazine wrote in 1872:

'It is impossible to put too many flounces, puffings and flowers on the . . . skirts of ball dresses.'

45. Day dress with apron-front over-skirt, 1875.

46. Evening dresses, 1870.

The Bustle Period

47. Evening dress with large bustle, 1887.

Outdoor Garments

All sleeved overcoats were figure-fitting and where necessary shaped to fit over the bustle.
The *Paletot* (for women) was long and sometimes trained, when worn with trained dresses.
The *Ulster*, common in the 1880's, was also long and had a belt. A cape was usual, or a hood hanging behind.
Sealskin jackets were so popular in 1875 that it was said that:

Women's Clothes

'the rage for sealskins has well nigh exterminated the seal'.

The *Dolman* was the most characteristic of this period (Fig. 48). It was a kind of mantle, with 'shawl' or 'sling' sleeves,

48. Mantles in the dolman style, 1879.

as they were called, which limited the movement of the arms to such an extent that 'a lady could scarcely blow her nose'.

Cloaks were also worn, made to fit at the shoulders.

The Bustle Period

Large fur muffs with a pocket for the card case were popular in the winter. Smaller muffs made of feathers, satin or velvet, sometimes trimmed with imitations of owls' heads, squirrels or kittens, were very fashionable.

Foot Wear

Day

Boots and shoes were similar to those in the last period, except that high heels were fashionable in the 1870's, coming down again in the 1880's.

Evening

Similar again to the last chapter, but evening boots were going out of fashion.

Stockings for afternoon wear were often coloured and embroidered up the front, such as:

'red silk stockings studded with swallows'.

Evening stockings were usually white, but black became the fashion for all stockings from 1888.

Head Wear

Indoors

Day. These caps were small and round or mere circles of lace worn flat on the head. Young women now wore nothing on their heads, and by 1887 indoor caps were only worn by the elderly.

Evening. Very small caps were worn chiefly as foundations for masses of trimming. Young women liked fancy combs or hair,

Women's Clothes

ornaments such as flowers, fruit, butterflies or even decorative insects!

Outdoors

Bonnets and hats were small in the 1870's (Fig. 49).

49. Polonaise dress. Very small hat on top of a large chignon. Man in lounge suit, 1872.

Hats were still considered a bit 'fast' but in 1878 it was stated that:

'when travelling, tourists may attend Divine Service in hats'.

The Bustle Period

After this hats began to rival bonnets, especially with the young. The hat with a very high crown, popularly known in the 1880's as the 'three storeys and a basement', pleased everyone.

Toques trimmed with fur were also fashionable, and *Tam-o'-Shanters*, *peaked jockey caps* and *boaters* were worn for outdoor activities. The top hat was correct for riding.

Again the trimming of hats and bonnets was often fantastic. A paper gave this description in 1885:

'Trimming of hats and bonnets include not only those insects and birds which appeal to our sense of beauty, but those which cause a revulsion of feeling such as spiders, water beetles, caterpillars and even lizards and toads.'

Doves, wings of pigeons and cockatoos were also popular and it was said that:

'Thirty thousand humming-birds are sometimes sold at the whole-sale auctions in an afternoon.'

Hair

Day and Evening

1870's. The front hair was turned back over a pad or 'frizzed', that is in tight curls. These were often artificial and gummed on to the forehead. The back hair was piled up into an enormous chignon (see p. 54) with the aid of masses of artificial hair. At this time shiploads were said to be imported.

1880's. A simpler coiffure was now the mode. The fringe, plain or 'frizzed', remained, but back hair was rolled into a bun at the back of the neck or on top of the head, which latter was more usual for the evening. Young women often

Women's Clothes

plaited their back hair into a loop hanging down, topped by a ribbon bow.

Make-up

This was used but it was bad taste for it to be obvious.

WOMEN'S CLOTHES
The Practical Period (1890's)

The next ten years show a struggle between physical freedom and fashionable femininity, so it became the mode to look tall and healthy and yet to retain a 19-inch waist.

Dresses

Day

The blouse and skirt for informal wear was now very usual (Fig. 50) and the tailor-made coat and skirt, or suit, was introduced for morning dress.

The *bodice* was figure-fitting in various designs.

Sleeves at first had a small 'kick-up' at the shoulders, but from 1893-7 the large 'leg-of-mutton' or 'gigot' sleeves were the ruling fashion (Fig. 51). They collapsed after 1897. The tea-gown continued to be worn for comfort and elegance.

Skirts. Double skirts soon vanished and various designs were made to make walking easier. All the new styles expanded downwards, but were still ground length.

Bloomers. The advent of the bicycle encouraged the wearing of knickerbockers, now often called bloomers (Fig. 52), and the more daring females wore them, sometimes with a Norfolk jacket and gaiters.

Women's Clothes

50. Blouse and skirt, 1896.

The Practical Period

Evening
The bodice was corset-like and very décolleté (Fig. 53). In 1897 it was said 'to hang on the shoulders by a miracle'. Short puffed sleeves were common and sometimes sleeves were replaced by mere shoulder straps. Skirts were always trained.
Boleros, which were very short jackets rounded to the bust, were sometimes worn with both day and evening dresses (Fig. 54).

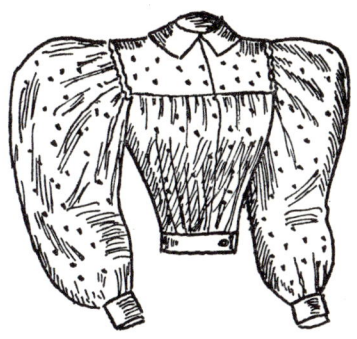

51. Morning blouse, 1894.

Favourite colours were yellow for the evening, and for day, mixtures of yellow, pink, green, red and orange.

Outdoor Garments

Cloaks and capes, long or short, were needed when gigot sleeves flourished (Fig. 55). When sleeves were narrow, figure-fitting long overcoats or jackets were preferred (Fig. 56).

A new style belonging to this period was the three-quarter length coat, which was worn whenever possible (Fig. 57).

Foot Wear

Day. Button boots or laced shoes or boots were usual, with high heels.
Evening. Low-cut slippers of leather or black satin with jewelled toe caps and also high heels were the mode.

Women's Clothes

52. Bicycling bloomers, generally known as 'rationals', 1896.

Stockings were generally black for day or evening, though some ladies wore coloured silk ones for evening.

Head Wear

Indoors
Day. Small oval caps raised in front were favoured by old ladies.
Evening. Decorative combs or ornaments of osprey or heron feathers were popular.

The Practical Period

53. Evening dress, 1894.

54. Blouse with bolero, 1899.

55. Cloak with deep cape, 1890.

Outdoors

Small bonnets were still worn by matrons, but were ceasing to be fashionable by 1898 'in spite of the patronage of Royalty'.

Toques continued.

Hats, small at first, were larger after 1897 when a fashion article stated that:

Women's Clothes

'all millinery may be described as rather gorgeous in colour and exuberant in decoration'.

Boaters and peaked caps were worn for outdoor exercise (Fig. 58). Veils were fashionable with hats and bonnets throughout this period.

Hair

The front hair had a wavy fringe or was brushed back from the forehead. The back hair was twisted into a bun, some-

56. Lady's short jacket, 1891.

57. Lady's three-quarter length overcoat, 1892.

The Practical Period

58. (a) Peaked cap, (b) boater, 1891.

times over a 'hair frame' to increase the size. The bun might be arranged at the back or on top of the head.

Women's hair was thick and long at this time, and many women could sit on their long tresses when they let them down.

Make-up

Any obvious make-up, especially rouge, was unladylike. The following incident is recorded of one of your author's forebears, a young lady with a very good complexion. She was out walking one day, when an impertinent young man turned to stare at her, remarking: 'Painted, by Jove.' She answered politely, 'No, Sir, by God.'

CHILDREN'S CLOTHES

Boys

Little boys were dressed like little girls up to the age of five or six, and then put into knickerbockers or trousers (Fig. 59). What was known as the 'Skeleton Suit' was very common until 1830. It consisted of trousers buttoned to and over a short close-fitting jacket worn with a wide white collar (Fig. 60).

59. Two little boys, 1896.

Children's Clothes

60. Little boy in skeleton suit, 1800.

61. Young boy in tunic and trousers, girls in frocks and frilled 'trousers', older boy in Eton jacket and trousers, 1840.

Children's Clothes

A tunic was more usual from the 1840's to 1860's. This was like a short overall with a belt. It was sometimes worn with white drawers instead of trousers by the very young (Fig. 61).

Older boys dressed like their fathers until the 1870's when knickerbockers and sailor suits (see Fig. 63c) were popular. For public school and formal wear tight, short black 'Eton jackets' with large white starched collars were the rule.

Girls

They followed the fashions of their mothers except that their dresses were shorter and, for the first half of the century, the wearing of white frilled drawers showing below the skirt was fashionable (Figs. 61 and 62).

62. Little girl with frilled drawers showing below her frock, *c.* 1826.

Boys and girls always had to wear some kind of head gear out of doors. In summer this was often a stiff straw sailor hat (see Fig. 63). A poor little girl who lost her hat in the zoo borrowed her brother's bowler hat, saying:

'I shall feel so ashamed going through the streets without a hat.'

The brother turned up the hood of his ulster so that his head too should be covered. In fact, formality was the order of the century (see Fig. 64).

63. (a) Girl aged 8 in princess frock; (b) girl aged 6 in pelisse with single cape; (c) 'A small British tar' in sailor suit and sailor hat, 1879.

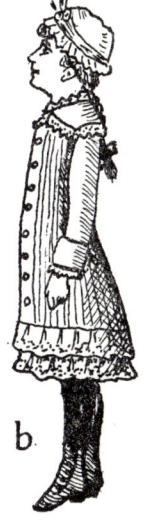

64. A visit to the Zoo.

INDEX

Apollo knot, 38, 39; *see* Hair styles
Aprons, 55

Bavolet, 36
Berets, 36
Bertha, 41
Blazer, 8
Bloomers, 49, 50, 67, 70
Blouse, 58, 67, 68, 69
Bolero, 69, 71
Bonnets, 29, 36, 43, 44, 53, 54, 64, 71; Spoon, 53
Boots, 18, 34, 44, 46, 50, 63; Button, 18, 69; Elastic-sided, 18, 19; Half, 29; Top, 18, 19, 26; Wellington, 18, 50, 51
Braces, 13
Breeches, 7, 11, 13
Bustle, 34, 41, 56, 61

Canes, 24
Caps, 29, 36, 44, 52, 59, 63, 70; Jockey, 65; Peaked, 72, 73
Chemise robe, 25
Chesterfield, 16, 17
Chignon, 53, 54, 64
Chin-stays, 36
Cloaks, 16, 17, 18, 27, 28, 50, 51, 62, 69, 71
Coats, 7, 69; Box, 16; Frock, *see* Frock coat; Morning, 7; Tail, 7, 9, 26

Collars, 13, 74, 76
Combs, 53, 63, 70
Cravat, 13
Crinoline, 47, 48, 49, 50, 56
Cummerbund, 10

Dolly Varden costume, 58, 59
Dolman, 62
Drawers, 76

Ear-rings, 55
Epaulettes, 47, 59
Eton jacket, 75, 76
Eyebrows, 55

Fall, 11
Feathers, 29, 39, 70; Feather pelerine, 42
Fig leaves, 55; *see* Aprons
Frock, 25
Frock coat, *frontispiece*, 7, 8, 9, 37

Gaiters, 19, 20, 29, 34, 67
Galoshes, 19, 44
Gloves, 24, 40, 41
Great coat, 16
Grecian bend, 25

Hair styles, 23, 24, 30, 38, 45, 65; American 21, 54; Hair frame, 73
Handbags, 40

78

Index

Hats, 20, 29, 44, 64, 71; Boaters, 65, 72, 73; Bollinger, 20, 22; Bowler, 20, 21, 76; Circumfolding, 23; Deer stalker, 23; Gibus, 23; Gipsy, 30; Glengarry, 54; Muffin, 20; Opera, 23; Pork-pie, 48, 54; Sailor, 76, 77; Straw, 21, 36, 39, 53, 54; Three storeys and a basement, 65; Top hat, 8, 20, 22; Trilby, 20
Hessians, 18
Highlows, 18, 29
Hooped skirt, 25

India-rubber, 44
Inexpressibles, 13
Inverness, 16, 17

Jackets, 7, 8, 22, 50, 69; Sealskin, 61
Jacket bodice, 21, 41, 42, 47, 48, 57, 58, 72, 74

Knickerbockers, 7, 8, 74, 76

Lounging jacket or lounge, 8, 11, 21, 64

Mackintosh, 16
Mantles, 27, 34, 50, 62
Mentonnières, 36, 37
Mob cap, 26, 29, 36
Muffs, 29, 34, 35, 63

Neckties, 13; Byron tie, 15
Nether integuments, 13
Norfolk jacket, 8, 12, 57, 58, 67

Octagon tie, 15, 16, *see* Neckties
Overcoats, 69, 72

Paletot, 16, 50, 51, 61
Pantaloons ('tights') 13; strapped, 8, 12
Parasols, 40
Pardessus, 42
Pattens, 29
Pelerine, 42
Pelisse, 27, 34, 77
Petticoat, 41, 47
Pockets, 40, 46
Poke bonnet, *frontispiece*, 9, 30
Polonaise, 58, 64
Princess dress, 59, 77
Pumps, 19

Rationals, 70
Reticules, 40, 46
Riding-habit, 50, 52
Rouge, 31, 39, 73
Ruff, *frontispiece*, 39

Sailor suit, 76, 77
Sandals, 29
Shawls, 9, 28, 34, 35, 42, 50
Shoes, 18, 19, 29, 46, 50, 63
Skeleton suit, 74, 75
Skirts, Apron-fronted, 21, 59, 60; Tie-backs, 56, 57
Sleeves, Beret, 33, 34; Detachable, 47; Gigot or Leg-of-mutton, 32, 37, 67
Slippers, 29, 34, 50, 69
Small clothes, 13, *see* Breeches
Spats, 20
Spatterdashes, 19
Spencer, *frontispiece*, 27, 28
Sticks, 24
Stock, 13
Stockings, 29, 50, 63, 70

Index

Surtout, 16

Tam-o'-Shanters, 65
Teagown, 59, 67
Tippets(capes), 34
Top frock or frock great coat, 16
Toques, 65, 71
Trimming, 56, 57, 63, 65; 'Follow-me-lads', 54
Trousers, 7, 11, 49, 74, 75, 76; Peg-top, 12; Railroad, 12; Strapped, *frontispiece*, 9, 11
Tunic, 75, 76
Tunic dress, 25, 26

Turban, 33, 36

Ugly, 44, 53, 54
Ulster, 16, 61, 76
Umbrellas, 24
Unmentionables, 13
Unwhisperables, 13

Veils, 36, 54, 72
Vest, 9

Waistcoat, 7, 9, 10, 12
Wigs, 23, 30

Ref.
GT
595
.C85